Tal

MW00904201

Just Steph Biography
Just Steph Products
Praise and Recommendations for Just Steph

Dedication

This book is dedicated to my father, Natty Palermo. Without him, not only would I not have life, but also I would have nothing about which to write. The dysfunction, insanity, tears and uncontrollable laughing fits are all owed to him. He loved frozen devil dogs, coaching Wellington-Glenwood Little League, and feeding his cats lobster. I hope you are cracking up in heaven, daddy. It's your time to be free.

Introduction

As a younger mom, I attended various talks designed to uplift me. Many targeted the often-discussed "mother role." The intent was for me to leave the workshop or retreat feeling empowered that I was forming the next generation of souls. I was supposed to feel good about wiping noses, cleaning vomit, managing the house and dealing with discipline issues that made me want to defect to Russia. I listened to the many stories from "holy" women chronicling their family lives. As great as my kids are, and as nice a life we lived, we never quite fit into the prescribed way of the "holy ones."

I always left somehow let down. How was I going to whip this family into shape? How was I going to live up to the St. Theresas who proclaimed that by submitting to church teachings and a simple life, my family would experience peace? This meant a life of complete piety, renouncing worldly goods and wearing clothes from the Amish country. Talk about keeping up with the Joneses...I was trying to keep up with the Marys, Marthas and Mother Teresas of the world. Why wasn't my husband more like St. Paul, St. Peter or the holy dads who attend bible studies?

I was smoking at the time. God forbid anyone found out. I would smoke all the way to these events, happy to get a break from kid central, and hope no one would come close to me. Of course, there was the obligatory hug. "Do you smell something burning?" I was an erupting volcano trying to subdue the pent-up F-bombs within. I'm Italian, from Boston. These church ladies were always so appalled at my blunt manner and my propensity to spout off bad language and improper innuendos at the drop of a dime. They would politely smile, maybe even chuckle, but then quickly excuse themselves from my presence. Was it something I said? I think I did it on purpose for the shock factor.

Ultimately, the outcome, for me, was wasted energy and feeling badly that I was a terrible wife, mother and person because I didn't fit in. This is exactly where I was comfortable. Let me explain. All my life I never felt part of the whole. I was different. I looked different (see "Let's Shake on it"), felt differently about myself (see "One Bad Apple Don't Spoil the Whole Bunch, Steph") and was raised in an environment that depended on family, food and gambling as the path to the happy place (see the rest of my pages). It wasn't the speakers' fault that I was not right. I needed to be me, comfortable with the gifts God has given me, including my family.

As a Monday-morning quarterback, I can preach: shoulda, coulda, woulda. Things could have been much different for me if only I had the understanding I do today. Hopefully in twenty years I can look back and say the same thing again because I will have grown even wiser. I tell you, until I looked down at the ruby slippers on my feet, I could not get off the treadmill of a life of both physical and emotional busy-ness (see "Jailhouse Rock"). I have everything necessary to live a balanced life filled with love for God and others as well as myself.

When I think about why I have compiled this book, I reason that I have come from a place of fear, self-loathing and self-neglect to one of contentment. I wanted to communicate this with you, your friends and anyone who will listen. I have come to realize that reflecting on my journey does not satisfy me. By sharing what's in my heart onto these pages, I experience a deeper healing and understanding of my life. I also can hold fast to the good and truly laugh out loud events in my Italian upbringing (see "The Ghost of Christmas Past"). Through my journey, I have discovered that a major source of pain for people, including myself, is disrespected personal boundaries. I have learned, and I hope I can share with you, how to establish healthy boundaries and stay consistent with them.

In the end, this book is as much for me as it is for all of you. I anticipate many editions to *The Only Way Is Up*, and hope you do as well. I truly desire to share my love with the world. If you have any questions or comments, please contact me at steph@juststeph.com.

I have divided *The Only Way is Up!* into parts: The Four Aspects, Italy, The Family, The Rise of Just Steph and Just Steph Today. My chapter topics overlap, but I have placed them where I think they belong. All comments, suggestions, and complaints will be read and considered, so let me know what you think!

Tell me what's going on in your life. I want to hear from you.

Wishing you love, balance and peace!

Amore & Baci (Love & Kisses),

Just Steph

The Four Aspects

Success is not measured by what we do or our material possessions, but by the healthy relationships in our lives. The means to healthy relationships are self-love and acceptance. This is achieved through balancing the physical, emotional, spiritual and intellectual aspects of the person. When one of these is lacking, we are surviving, not thriving.

Physical- The physical aspect is the easiest to identify. When we live an unhealthy lifestyle, with a poor diet and a lack of exercise and sleep, our bodies suffer. This, in turn, contributes to low energy, poor self-esteem, and other medical issues. Inadequate self-discipline in the physical area of our lives can lead to lack of self-worth and even depression. I can help you harness this discipline to gain a more positive self-image and dignity.

Emotional- The emotional aspect is harder to grasp. We can, on the outside, seem functional, happy, even peaceful. We become great pretenders. Each one of us has a deep need to spend time with family, friends, and our spouse or significant other. We desire to be accepted, feel like we belong, experience dynamic friendships and be encouraged and challenged to grow and change. Through discussions and suggested reading and documenting daily life situations, together we can identify areas that need attention.

Intellectual- If we are not moving forward, we are going backwards. We have the capacity to continually learn new ideas. The intellectual aspect, when thriving, breaks down racial barriers and prejudices through expanding our world beyond ourselves. We need to be challenged to raise our standards, read things that challenge us as well as feed our professional and entertainment interests. Together, we will outline your interests and find ways to extend your intellectual world.

Spiritual- The spiritual aspect helps us to understand the other three areas. We all desire peace in our world. Contributing to the happiness of others gives us a sense of purpose. Whether we know it or not, each person needs silence, solitude and simplicity. Taking advantage of the three S's will help us to focus on where you need to improve. I can help you to find time for the three S's and decipher what is realized once you have incorporated them into your life.

The following chapters speak to the four aspects of the human person. I believe balancing these four aspects, which is a continual journey, brings peace. We can, though, advance and experience true peace and self- acceptance as we advance toward

perfect balance.

Burning the Candle at Both Ends

I am just about to board my plane heading back to Atlanta from Boston. Every year I get home from Boston and hit the wall. I get a full-blown cold and sinus infection, swine flu or some other ailment. In his book *Choice Theory*, author William Glasser says we choose to be sick. Sounds crazy, right? I don't want to be sick; I don't choose the bacteria and viruses that infect me, do I? Hear me out:

I just spent the last ten days running around like a twenty-one-year old, eating, drinking, dancing and hanging out until the wee hours catching up with old friends. I am bloated, swollen, exhausted and flabby. I have depleted my immune system, not to mention the adrenaline that kept me going like the Energizer Bunny is now on empty. Of course I'm going to get sick. I feel it already: scratchy throat, fatigue, sinus pressure.

So whether you are worn out by your stressful, hectic everyday life, or you are trying to relive your twenties, don't expect to feel good. Don't go around blaming the other people or the dirty shopping cart for your cold. Take a good look at how you are living and make some changes. Serious illnesses like cancer can be attributed to stress as well as poor living. Exercising, eating healthy, avoiding poisons like alcohol and drugs (I know you are overimbibing and smoking whatever), keeping stress levels low and getting proper rest will add years to your life. Believe it or not, you will have more energy and feel great.

So hopefully, I can follow my own advice and hit it hard when I land in Atlanta. I had a blast in Boston. Unfortunately, I will probably do the same thing next year. But at least I can blame myself for being sick when I get home.

Don't Go Breaking My Heart

The heart is fragile. It has a mind of its own. The heart is constantly seeking to be loved and filled up. When the heart is neglected, especially for a long period of time, it runs amuck. The heart will take you anywhere to satiate itself. Who is responsible for this neglect? We can blame our parents, siblings, the mean kids with whom we attended school, our spouses or even our kids. But who is really to blame here? Ourselves! We are at the helm of our own happiness.

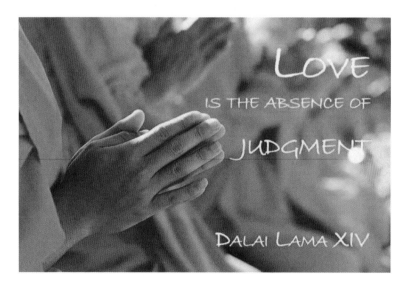

I am in charge of my heart, not the other way around. I make the choices to believe the lies people tell me about how I don't measure up, that I am ugly, worthless, unlovable, etc. I make the choice to take the actions of another as a rejection of me. I make the choices to react to this treatment in such a way that I end up looking for love in all the wrong places.

When we don't live a physically healthy lifestyle, the results are easy to recognize. A deficiency in emotional well-being is not so easy to distinguish. Early action is necessary before things blow up on you. Reevaluate unproductive, dysfunctional relationships. Do you have someone that loves you unconditionally, with whom you can be your total self? Are you taking time to nourish your heart with good self-help books, therapist, Al-Anon or AA? When was the last time you laughed until you cried?

Think about all these things before your heart brings you down a road of no return.

Ditch All the Stuff

Our lives have become so cluttered with stuff. We are bogged down with having to have it all, keeping up with the Jones, the latest and greatest. We don't talk anymore. I remember as a kid just sitting around after dinner talking and laughing, playing cards and board games. Now my kids are texting me from the other room to see what's for dinner. NO social skills. People wonder why they are miserable. Everyone is behaving like they are on their own deserted island. We were created by God to exist in community. We are supposed to be social and to support one another in joys and sorrows. Now we are texting people our condolences for a loss instead of bringing over a meal and sitting down to lend an ear or picking up the phone to talk.

Ditch the stuff, people! Interact with each other. Talk with your loved ones. Put on the coffee and enjoy one another.

Jailhouse Rock

An old friend posted this on Facebook today, "For the first time ever, I looked into the mirror and said out loud: 'you deserve better'...I nearly had an out-of-body experience and scared myself!" This is her get-out-of-jail-free card. Will she use it or remain in her comfy cell? We are inmates who are assigned to the chain gang of psychological dysfunction. We work it every day, moaning and groaning our lives away while we try to convince ourselves we are happy.

We neglect ourselves emotionally as we do physically. We eat poorly, refuse to exercise and don't sleep well. Our bodies' screams for help manifest as fatigue, extra weight, high blood pressure, yet even as we hear the cries for change, we do not always listen. The psyche is no different, just harder to recognize, and even more difficult to modify. It is so much easier to remain in prison. It's secure, we know the rules, we have no rights, we are not important, and we are nice and cozy. We don't even have to look in the mirror; there isn't one for fear we may use it to hurt ourselves or someone else.

The emotional prison is both inflicted on us and self-imposed. Incarceration begins when we are very young. We are told one way or another to behave a certain way or risk losing people. The actions of those around us instill fear in us. Toe the line or risk abandonment, rejection, humiliation. We choose to keep these beliefs into adulthood. It's safe there. I know the outcome. I believe the lies. As a young mother, I neglected my body, heart and dreams because I was not worth the effort. If I took care of myself, I have to say, yes, I deserve better. I did not believe I merited anything.

What does it mean to break free from this prison? First and foremost, I need to recognize I am in solitary confinement, and my thought processes may be distorted. I choose to remain alone in the cell or to bust out. The challenge is in the escape. It can be painful. We need to see where we have fallen short, where others have let us down and that we have choices. I am worth a happy and fulfilling life. I have something to give back to the world, and the world has something for me.

Next we need to stop believing the lies. The falsehoods from life situations can be devastating. What do I mean by this? We are trained from a young age to buy into and live by a set of beliefs that are simply untrue. We perceive every painful event as a validation for these beliefs. We can say, "See, I am not worth it, I am ugly, I am not smart enough." But we will continue to suffer the same pain over again until we change our perspective and realize: it's not about me! The people to whom we choose to listen may need to be varied. I have found that aligning myself with good, honest friends and mentors who uplift me as well as help me to see where I need improvement offset those negative vibes from the not-so-do-gooders. I can be my own worst enemy. I need to stop listening to my own Debbie Downer comments as well. My responsibility lies in doing the next right thing to the best of my ability.

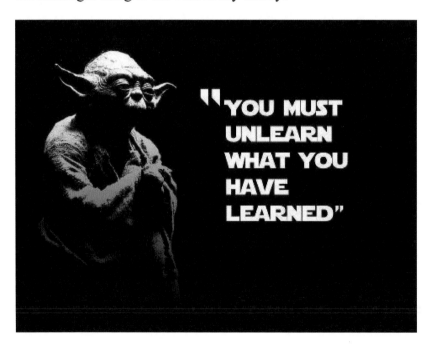

Finally, it's time to enjoy the new-found energy that we used to expend to keep us in the dark cell. It's time to bask in the sunlight of a new day. It is surprising how much energy I spent worrying about how I could justify myself and my actions, that I was ok. I really was only trying to convince myself anyway. I now have a renewed sense of self. I am relishing my life: starting a new business, meeting new people, living life on life's terms. The burden is so much lighter. Stop the skipping LP in your head. Records are so 1970's; leave yours there too. Look in the mirror and say out loud: "I deserve better!"

The Best Things in Life Are Free

They say (I don't know who "they" are) there's no such thing as a free lunch. As usual, I disagree. One of the most profound ways we can grow spiritually, regardless of our religious affiliation, is to give back to the community. "Giving back to the community" needs further exploration and clarification.

Let's define community. In my opinion, community refers to any person or organization that is in our individual sphere of reality. Our higher power places people and opportunities in our path for a reason. All are stepping-stones on the journey toward truly becoming ourselves, guiding us closer to our own fulfillment and the eternal bliss in the afterlife. Each day provides a plethora of encounters from which we can grow spiritually by receiving the gift from someone or sharing what we have with "our community." Our community can include, but is in no way limited to, spouses, family members, our social circle and local charities. When we do good deeds, we share a piece of the eternal. We present God to the world. The hopeless and despairing experience hope. The lonely now have a friend. The lost are found. The sick are healed. The depressed touch joy, and the hungry are fed.

So what exactly is "the gift?" The gift is very simply put, me and you. It is sharing who we truly are and our unique talents. Our present to the world, ourselves, originates from real love. We must be willing to allow ourselves to be a bit vulnerable. In order to have the courage to expose ourselves, the love must flow from the abyss within that is our higher power. There are no strings attached. When we impart our gifts to others, we receive back as much or more than we give. Our motivation comes from the understanding that the other person is worth it. They deserve our gift of self. Ironically, it is here, in the giving, that the giver is the one who advances on the stepping-stones of life, maybe even more than the receiver.

Last night, my husband and I had the opportunity to give back. We attended an event to benefit the Atlanta Food Bank, which provides food and supplies to millions of people around north Georgia. One of our dear friends, who, incidentally is the Governor of Red Sox Nation for the state of Georgia, was roasted along with two other restaurateurs. I feel, as does my husband, truly blessed to be able to make a contribution to this wonderful charity. My favorite way to give back to my community, however, is to love the individuals that God places in my world. I enjoy lifting their spirits and touching their hearts. This is where I am most vulnerable, and when I am most rewarded. Try it! Your world is waiting for you.

The most important thing in life is to learn how to give out love, and let it come in.

~ Mitch Albom

JOHN EDWARD .NET

All I Want For Christmas Is...

Tradition, as defined in my iPhone dictionary app, is a specific practice of long standing and/or an inherited pattern of thought or action. Basically, traditions are those rituals we perform over and over through the years and pass down to our kids. We may tweak what our parents did or start new ones. Traditions are like mac and cheese, comfort food for our souls. They make us feel safe and secure. We know what will happen next. The traditions with which I was raised and even those I started fresh with my family make me feel like I am wrapped in a Boston Red Sox Snuggie while lying on the couch watching Jaws for the umpteenth time.

I asked various friends and family to share their favorite traditions with me.

Gigi from Atlanta, GA, emailed and said," What comes to mind for me is that my mom passed on her recipes to me and now I make and share them with my kids. Holidays were very special at my house and now my kids love the same foods and traditions. In so many ways I feel like my parents are with us celebrating."

Natalie from Wakefield, MA, responded to my Facebook request, "Here's something I remember well.....my sister never helped clear the table on any holiday....NEVER." (If you haven't guessed, Nat is my sister.)

Camille from Peabody, MA, also via FB, tells us about her father's nuts, "My favorite tradition is my father roasting his nuts every Thanksgiving. We get the biggest laugh when we have to call him to check his nuts. By the way, he's 95."

Christine from Santa Fe, TN, writes in on FB about her Italian Christmas Eve: "One of my favorite memories involved our traditional Italian Christmas Eve dinner, known as The Feast of Seven Fishes. We always had family and friends around to share the food, love and joy of being together. A family friend we called Uncle Walter always told the same stories every year. We humored him every year as if it were the first time we had heard each one. One year, my brother Ross and I were standing at the kitchen sink clearing things for the next course while Uncle Walter started one of his repeats. We both--simultaneously--were able to mouth the exact words he was saying. We could not stop laughing at the fact that we had both managed to memorize his story. For the rest of the evening, it became a private joke between the two of us, and we still laugh about it to this day."

Merry Christmas and Happy New Year! Make 2013 a year of self-fulfillment.

Italy

I traveled to Italy and Sicily for two weeks this past September. Touring the ancient cities and countryside caused me reflect on what is truly important. Visiting the cathedrals, basilicas, burial places of the holy ones and the towns where my family once lived evoked emotion, nostalgia and a longing for simplicity. Finding my family in Riesi, Sicily, rekindled an appreciation for my family and the traditions with which I was raised.

During my trip, I was struggling with serious personal issues. Those issues together with my experiences produced the following chapters. I wanted to publish my lamentations. Someday I may be able to commit my conflicts to paper. For now, I want to write out of love, not anger. When I can articulate my battles without accusation and with personal acceptance, I will share my heart. For now, you have what I believe benefits you and me.

Know that what I shared on each page emerged from my weary heart. I worked diligently to produce positive ideas from a dark, negative solitude. Just Steph is not normally an unhappy person. I hate the pain of depression, self-loathing and misery. If you receive any light from my overseas texts, thank God! He brought forth something good from a dispiriting situation. In fact, one of my favorite chapters is "We Are Family. I've Got All My Cousins With Me." There is a quote in that passage I know came from my higher power. I was shocked when I wrote it. Enjoy what was produced during my travels.

Put the Shoe on the Other Foot

Our first night in Rome, my husband and I walked about an hour and a half looking for Taverna Trilussa, the restaurant for which we had reservations. When we finally made it, I had a blister the size of a Kennedy half-dollar. For me, though, it's fashion over comfort. Dinner was amazing, but we took a cab back to the hotel.

The next day, as we toured the Coliseum, Pantheon, Trevi Fountain and other sights, I was forced to think about my feet and my shoes. I also thought about the life of the ancients. What was it like for them? It was a much simpler existence. Walking was the primary mode of transportation. The roads were not nicely paved, so their shoes must have been simple sandals that were flexible, unlike my stilettos from the night before. Food was simple, all clean eating: olives, fruit, vegetables, olive oil, simple breads and the like. They had conversations, talking in the Forum. They met their friends and relatives to tell them any news, no phones, texting or Internet.

The other idea that has stuck with me in this journey is the benefits of travel. Matthew Kelly, author of *The Rhythm of Life*, has this to say about travel: "Travel opens our minds to different cultures, philosophies, and world views. Travel opens our hearts to the people of foreign lands and their different traditions and creeds. Travel dissolves the stains of prejudice that infect our hearts and societies. Money spent on travel is money well spent on an education that you will never receive from a book or in a classroom."

I loved this when I read the book. It has stuck with me. I wanted to share with all of you. When we journey to other countries, or even different parts of our own country, we enter into solidarity with those who live there. This in itself encourages the breakdown of racial barriers and prejudices. So in essence, when we visit another country, we walk in others' shoes for the duration of our stay. We experience their lives, what it's like for them every day.

So put the shoe on the other foot and get out of your comfort zone. Visit new places, meet the people and experience new cultures. I am getting on a plane to visit my family's homeland, Sicily. I will keep you posted.

<u>Who's Sorry Now?</u>

If you believe in a higher power, at some point you will fall short. You will do something that offends God and probably hurts yourself and someone you love. So what to do? Well this morning I landed in the eternal city. That's right, Rome, Italy. What better place to face my God but the burial place of hundreds of popes and many saints, St. Peter's Basilica?

Non-Catholics, bear with me. Like I said, at some point you need to say sorry to God for what you have done. I have chosen the "Mecca" for Catholics...the Vatican. There are confessionals along the sides of St. Peter's where you can confess your sins in any language. I approach the English confessional and enter. I confess my sins as bluntly as I do anything. That's my personality. I know God already knows. What's there to hide? I might as well let it all out. So I did. The priest was lovely and sweet, very caring. I said my Act of Contrition and he offered me a prayer card with a relic of Blessed Pope John Paul II. So why did I not feel better? Why was my burden not lifted from me? I said my penance prayers. Why do I still walk around heavy?

I believe it is because we are all cracked eggs. We come into relationships already cracked. When we hurt each other our cracks get larger. We can be sorry all we want. We can even try to make "real" amends. But the truth is, what's done is done. This is why God doesn't really need to punish us. We suffer the consequences of our own sins. It's called "free will." We did it, God sadly watched and now we suffer. We suffer and the people around us suffer.

So how do we rectify this situation? How do we rise up? I tell you now: God has already forgiven and has moved on. He wants you and me to move on. God has forgotten. But we as cracked eggs have a very hard time moving on, and maybe rightfully so. The standard is to look at God, your higher power and emulate Him. Work toward moving on, forgiving, forgiving yourself, accepting your part in the wrong-doing and trying to do better next time.

We need to look at those mistakes, the cracks, and learn from them, embrace them and turn things around to do good for your loved ones and neighbors. No matter how you feel, know your higher power loves and forgives you. My God loves me; can I love myself?

Keep up with me as I travel through Italy and Sicily. I will keep you posted on what I am doing and hopefully inspire you to make positive changes in your life.

Mangiamo! (Let's Eat!)

There are two activities that God created both pleasurable and necessary for human survival. Eating is one of them. You can deduce the other. Mealtime, throughout history, has been portrayed in books, poetry, music and art. Food is referenced innumerable times in Sacred Scripture, and most importantly in the meal of meals, the Last Supper.

For me, every meaningful event in my life has been surrounded with fabulous delicacies. Even sad events like funerals included a gathering between viewing times and ended with a large gathering at a local restaurant for the final event. This helped us through the grief, being with the people closest to the deceased and us. We even had a good laugh, telling funny memories of our loved ones.

I never thought I was an emotional eater. I didn't eat when I was lonely, depressed or angry. It took me four years of taking care of my diet to realize I am, in fact, an emotional eater. I eat to get to the happy place, my happy place. The happiest part of the day was always dinner. No matter how bad things were growing up, we sat down to dinner, talked and laughed. We could hardly wait to break bread with our cousins at the holidays.

Today, I am still trying to get to that happy place. It's about the party, the feel good. I love feeding anyone who enjoys great food. I love everything about food, the aromas, flavors, textures, the wine, the company and the ambience. Although the experience is always enjoyable, I can never quite reach my "real" happy place. The food never quite does it. In the end, when I overdo it, I feel worse about myself for not having control. I then have to spend most of the week trying to undo the damage from the weekend.

I have to say, my travels through Italy and Sicily have been a culinary explosion and we are only a quarter of the way through. I have enjoyed every morsel of every meal. My stomach kills, but I will probably not skip the next meal out of fear that I will miss something. I am scared to see how tight my clothes might be by the end of this trip, but it will be well worth it. The olive oil, cheeses and pasta are all fabulous.

Who knows, maybe I will find my happy place here in the motherland. I found my cousins in Reisi. So anything is possible. I will be posting some photos and videos of this wonderful event as well as some others. Keep reading! I will be catching up with you again soon!

Pass the Flux Capacitor

Sicily is an amazing place. It's as if time has stopped. Cell phone coverage is sporadic, at best, internet access is impossible unless your hotel provides service and air conditioning is a commodity. I have stepped into a time warp. Traveling through the towns of my ancestors, I have found that traditions have not changed. It felt as though I sat in the DeLorean with Michael J. Fox and we went back in time.

The people of Sciacca still have a deep devotion to Madonna del Soccorso. In mid–August, they celebrate her feast day and the fishermen carry the statue of the saint on their backs throughout the town, much like the Italian feasts in Boston. For a funeral, they carry the casket from the church to the cemetery, just like what we see in "The Godfather."

In Sciacca, I found the records of my great-grandparents, Cologero LaRosa and Caterina Piazza. I found out their dates of birth, addresses and parents' names. All these records were in handwritten ledgers in a building that was hundreds of years. The women helping me were so cute. Because my great-grandparents' last names are so common, it would take days to find living relatives.

So I took down all the information I could and moved on to the nearest ceramic shop for a reminder of my visit.

We found the most amazing sculpture of Madonna del Soccorso being carried by at least 30 fisherman. We met the artists and visited their studio. They told us about the statue. I cannot wait to display this beautiful piece of my heritage in my home.

More meaningful than any souvenir, what I will leave Sciacca with is a renewed belief in simplicity and a reaffirmed sense of what's really important. Staying connected to the world via technology is not a priority for them. Their families, their crafts and devotion to God through the Madonna are their lives. Distractions are minimal. Conversing over espresso in the square is the highlight of their day. They interact and socialize face to face.

I hope I can live what I have learned.

We Are Family! I've Got All My Cousins With Me!

God has created us to live in community. Socializing first occurs immediately after birth with our mother as she holds and feeds her newborn. This is our first sense of security and comfort. Our world then extends to fathers, siblings and later extended family. It is here that we learn to love and be loved. Our family environment teaches how to live out the four aspects of the human person: physical, emotional, spiritual and intellectual.

We come to understand the importance of mealtime (or the lack thereof) as not only a time of nourishment, but socialization. The types of food we enjoy become part of who we are. Do we finish our plate because there are starving children in China? Do we eat until we burst or until we are satisfied? Are we ridiculed for eating too much or not eating enough? Is mealtime pleasant? A time for sharing the day's events? These and many more set the stage for how we treat our bodies regarding food.

Growing up, I also noticed that families as a whole may or may not have been physically active. You could look at a family and know they were either playing sports or watching TV. Sports and exercising were not a priority in my house. Finding a physical activity I loved as well as making workouts a priority was challenging and took a long time to develop. Today, my family skies every year together, even though I would still rather park my butt at the beach with my mojito. Our annual ski trip is something we cherish and do together.

Emotionally, we come to understand appropriate displays of affection, core beliefs, manners and what is socially acceptable. We also learn how we should be treated and how to treat others, especially those closest to us. If we were constantly teased, rejected, abandoned, uplifted or loved unconditionally, that is what we will swallow and regurgitate. How our parents treated each other, for example, is how we will treat our spouses, even unconsciously. Of course, some events are subtle and others extreme like physical abuse. *No matter, the family exhales its emotional fumes that fill our very being with the second-hand smoke from our environment that can either slowly kill us or breathe life into our souls.*

Poor God! The family is the domestic church. It is here that we learn the basis for our religious and spiritual beliefs. Our parents (sorry, but in most cases, ugh!) are our mirror image of God. Think about the characteristics you have ascribed to God. Is he ever an ever-present, loving, protecting provider? Or is he absent, mean, judgmental, distant? Think about who raised you. There is a good chance some or most of these attributes are the same.

Was school important in your family? Reading? Were you encouraged to pursue your creative dreams? Was it over-emphasized? Did we let our parents down when we didn't make the grades? How we feed our brain with good information also stems from what we learned at home. Not getting a college degree was not an option for me. But I was never encouraged to pursue my dreams, whatever they were. I needed to get my degree, get a job, find a husband and settle down. None of this is bad in it of itself, but was this the whole picture for me? I can tell you no. As you see, I am 45 and just starting to find out what my dreams really are.

For Italians, the family is the primary social circle. The family always comes first (which I still believe in today). Sunday dinners are the event of the week. Baptisms, birthdays, weddings, wakes and funerals are all family affairs for us. This is so important to me, I set out to find living relatives in Sicily. God blessed me with a new extended family. I found my cousins in Reisi. What a great day this was. I could hardly speak. They are intending to invite my husband and me to my cousin's wedding next year in Catania; such a blessing. I love my family. My extended family of cousins brought so much joy into my life; I almost jump out of my skin when I know we are getting together. Now I have a new set of cousins. Enjoy some of my photos.

The Family

Italian families are known for being loud, loving and well fed. Mine was no different. We say what's on our minds, regardless of who's present, and we are fiercely loyal. I could have a knock-down, drag-out F-you fight with any one of my friends or family. In my next breath, I promise, I would go to the grave in their defense. I have experienced that first-hand with my sister. I told her a few years back that someone told me he didn't like me. She said, "Did you tell him you didn't f@#king like him or his whore mother?" I have many other stories like this, but I don't want to scare you.

Twenty-one years ago, shortly after the birth of my first baby, my husband and I moved from Boston, then to Southern California, and we finally settled in Atlanta. None of my family or friends could understand why we would leave home. "Shteeeph, what's in Jawjah (Georgia)? You like it there? When you comin' home?" This was one of the most difficult life events I have experienced. Birthing three babies sans drugs was easier. My heart was broken. Anytime my mom visited, I had a perpetual lump in my throat for days after she left. Very rarely did anyone else visit. The

Boston crowd doesn't leave home, their mother or Sunday dinner for anybody.

It took me seven years to call Georgia my home. I love it here, but it just isn't my "'hood." I will always miss Boston, holidays with my family and the call saying, "Put the coffee on. I'm on my way." I miss the laughing 'til it hurts with my cousins. They get me and I get them. Periodically, I need a Boston fix. I just wish someone would come visit me.

I trust you will get a feel for how it was for me growing up. Maybe, if I become famous, my family will finally come visit. It's doubtful. They don't care where I live, what I weigh, who my friends are and how big my house is. They love me for me. They just will not leave Boston.

The Ghost of Christmas Past

Arriving on the heels of the Christmas Eve seafood extravaganza was the day for which we had all been preparing. The smell of meatballs basking in Filippo Berio, eggplant parm in the oven, veal cutlets waiting on the meatballs to vacate the olive-oil-laden fry pan, antipasto, ravioli as well as all the American traditional holiday fare were signs that Christmas had arrived. The aroma of garlic was imbedded in every porous surface of our small five-room flat.

Of course Santa's sleigh had tipped over our living room where my sister and I, in the wee hours, tore through every Barbie accessory known to man. With all the toys, new clothes and gold chains, my sister and I chomped at the bit for the best part of the day. The most exciting, highly anticipated event would be when all my aunts, uncles and cousins would march into the house demanding a dish of macaroni (not to be confused with mac and cheese).

We ate from one end of the house to the other. My father had inevitably invited some stranger to dine with us. Everyone would look down to the end of the table and say who the f@#k is that? We were so lucky to have had three grandparents, our great-grandmother and our great-uncle at the Christmas table until my

early twenties. The older generation only spoke broken English, a

mix between Sicilian, English and Bostonese: "Heyya, who'sa the

cavona downa dere?" Translation: Hey, who's the pig down there?

After everyone got over the weirdo at the table, it was time to

settle our coulos (bum, ass) into the throne where we would spend

the next several hours eating course after course. Many of our

family friends would stop by from early evening into the night filling

the house until it split at the seams. Just when the brioschi (an old-fashioned remedy for heartburn) was working, my mother would clear dessert and re-serve whatever could be placed in a spucki (that's delicious Italian bread, by the way): cutlet, ham, turkey & capicola sandwiches for everyone!

We ate and laughed, ate and laughed all day and night. We always played a game like Trivial Pursuit, which my grandmother never wanted to play, but yelled out every answer from her end of the table. Those were the days. No matter how bad things got throughout the year, Christmas with my cousins was the summit of joy, peace, love, safety and the ultimate crack up. My husband and four boys left Boston for the land of milk and honey, the Bible belt, that is. We now spend Christmas with dear friends and decadent rib roasts. We may even enjoy Christmas dinner out at a fancy hotel on occasion.

If only my grandmother could see and experience the life I live today. She would be shocked and maybe even disappointed that there's no lasagna or cannoli at Christmas. Today, I have help with keeping up the house and live the American dream. So why the tears this Christmas? I long for Christmas past with my cousins and endless hours of talking and laughing with the only ones who understand what it all means to me.   I guess I just miss my family.

 Maybe it was just easier when my mother handled all the details of

Christmas while my sister and I just had to be there to enjoy it all.

Thanks to all of you for giving me a place to relive my Christmas

past. Merry Christmas to you all. May you find the warmth I

enjoyed nestled at the perpetual feast of feasts. God Bless!

What's the Spread?

Americans live for Super Bowl Sunday. Newly made
resolutions to diet, exercise, watch less TV, and stop dropping the F-
bomb are swept under the ottoman. Instead, the 30-day health
regimen succumbs to Buffalo wings and nachos, permanent ass
indents on the couch, a day full of football reruns and commentaries
and cursing at refs and bad plays since before the Joe Namath days.

Growing up with the TV next to the dining room table during
football season, my sister and I developed a great disdain for
football. We ate Sunday dinner at half-time of one game, then my
dad would reach over and change the channel to one of the other two

channels to catch the other scores. Sunday dinner was a celebration of whatever my mother had been slaving over all morning. It always included meatballs and whatever pasta my father desired that day, as well as some other sides that Americans referred to as a main course like roasted chicken, veal cutlets, pork loin, etc. Football season put a damper on our weekly feast.

My dad sat on the edge of the couch every weekend anxiously awaiting the outcome of the teams on which he had gambled. We had no reprieve. The Blue Law prevented us from escaping to the mall. By Sunday night, we knew if we had to eat at my grandmother's that week or if Big Nat was taking us to Tello's in East Boston for a new pair of Jordache jeans. It was a bad weekend when he had to get on a chair and pull the wads of cash out of the dropped ceiling.

The menu on Super Bowl Sunday was different from other Sundays for us. Chinese was the fare. Egg rolls, lobster sauce, pork fried rice, chicken fingers and *REAL* duck sauce (NO PACKETS!!!!) were just a small sampling. Bostonians love Chinese; Cantonese, that is. Although the day was another "holiday" for us, my sister and I jumped for joy when the Blue Law was overturned. We could now hit the mall while my father chomped at the bit over the spread, the football cards and what he might owe on collection day.

Today, we celebrate Super Bowl Sunday Boston style with a hint of living south of the Mason-Dixon Line: great food, fab friends, oversized Patriots blow-up figures on the lawn and a once-a-year pool heating. With a husband and four sons (three of which play football), I have had to suppress the bad memories of my childhood football experience and instead enjoy the day all Americans anticipate, Super Bowl Sunday. Go Pats!

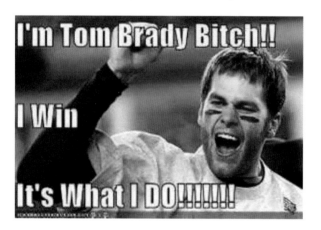

The American Nightmare

I grew up just outside Boston, Medford (Meffa), in a neighborhood where the houses looked like Archie Bunker's. We were pretty much low-income, except when my father hit it big on a football game, and we looted the mall with a vengeance before the well ran dry. I slept in the same bed as my sister, and we ate from one end of the house to another at the holidays. Sometimes, my grandmother had to buy our groceries after a weekend of sports upsets.

We rented our apartment from Italian immigrants who barely spoke English. The dad screamed at me one day when I was attempting to make a snowman. The bottom got too big to push out of the driveway so I listened to him berate me with Italian cursing like stupida (stupid) and disgratiata (disgrace). There was a boy, my age, who lived upstairs. He liked to use me as a punching bag every once in a while, not to mention the name calling. We couldn't play in the yard; the whole thing was a vegetable garden. Space for my sister and me was very limited. We played at the park all day every summer. Harris Park was our vacation destination.

All of our extended family and friends owned their own homes. The kids had their own rooms and space to play. My sister and I watched the American Dream unfold before us; we were spectators. When my father finally raked in enough dough to buy a house, we moved to north Meffa only to have the house repossessed by the bank after a lengthy losing streak. Devastating! My heart went from longing, to ecstatic, to broken by the time I turned eighteen.

I was going to have a home, a yard, and space for my kids to play. My husband and I bought our first home in Woodstock, GA. I thought I hit the number: four bedrooms, two and a half baths, a cul-de-sac and neighbors who resembled human beings, but I later realized a few of them were aliens from Bizarro World. Where the Hell did we land this spaceship? New Hampshire?

Fast forward two houses and three moves later. We put our kids in a school in Atlanta and decided to move to the big city. Thank God! The country was killing me. We built the dream house. The Beverly Hillbillies loaded up the truck and moved to Buckhead, several bathrooms, karaoke bar, swimming pool, fancy neighbors. Do you think that stopped me from screaming at the top of my lungs to the kids on the front yard: "Get in the house. It's time for suppaah!?" My neighbors thought Fran Drescher moved in. Southerners cannot differentiate the accents, BTW.

So did the big house make me happy? Ha! Every time something breaks, we drop a fortune. Yes, you heard me, big bucks. My husband bought the insurance policy with a very large deductible to save money. Recently, the tree roots suffocated our sewerage pipes, backup in the basement: cha ching! Lightning hit our yard. The sound system blew: $$$$. The roof on our first home that is now a rental needs replacing: WTF! My husband needs three teeth implants: ugh! "Can we get a Groupon for your teeth, dear?"

I am ready to ditch it all and move to an apartment. I want one kitchen, one living room and Carlton your door man. I long to walk to the coffee shop and stumble home after a few vodkas at my fav city spots. I'm anticipating the true American Dream: freedom.

For now, though, it's the money pit for us. My kids love the house. There isn't a weekend that goes by that I don't get woken up at four a.m. by kids screaming over Ping-Pong and insist that they find a bed somewhere, just not my room or my mother's. I watch my husband every Saturday on the mower (yes, we manicure our own lawn: remember we are the Griswalds) talking out his upcoming week with himself. How can I take this away from them? After all, we are living the American Dream.

The Rise of Just Steph

In my introduction, I described what it was like for me to attend motivational talks as a young mother. I always wondered how these speakers could dig up so many personal experiences. When I reflected on this, I thought I had nothing from my life to give to anyone. I was so blocked. I couldn't see my own beauty, and I didn't even know there was pain.

Talk about denial! I was in the dark. I was numb from the neck up. I submerged myself into bottles, diapers, nail clipping and the inflexible daily routine. I was caring for all the needs of everyone else. I never even thought I was neglecting myself. After all, I was eating more calories than a truck driver. I made sure I got to bed early enough. I was so anal about my kids' bedtime. I retired every evening worried that this was going to be the night one of them woke with some illness and I would be deprived of my beauty sleep. Everyone to bed by seven o'clock p.m.!

It never occurred to me that if I took care of me, everyone else would be better for it. My boys would have an example of a mom who knew her own dignity. Instead of self-loathing and self-destruction, they would witness self-love and respect. Today there would be less resistance to my new found, better self. I have shocked the system.

The following chapters are my attempt at being a Monday-morning quarterback. I have looked in the rearview mirror. Recounting my life experiences, I express my perspective then and what it all means to me now. As I spilled my heart in these posts, I was liberated and healed. I am forever grateful to my loyal readers and those who encouraged me. It was confirmation that I was on the right track.

Welcome Back, Kotter (Steph)

Welcome back, my dreams were my ticket out...I left Boston over 20 years ago and built a new life with my young family. I lived on both coasts until settling in Atlanta where my husband built his business while I made the land where the peaches grow our home. As I think about what it is I want to convey to all of you, I am flooded with emotion. I left the warm cocoon of my family where I am loved unconditionally, never judged and most importantly woke to the smell of meatballs frying every Sunday.

My besties are an extension of my family. We have been going out dancing since the CYO days when Donna Summer's "Last Dance" was a new release. We had each other's back. We were like glue. We always had the crack up. We were all raised very similarly, and their mothers fried meatballs on Sunday morning too. It was the days of carefree fun.

As I raised my family, I lost the sense of closeness I felt with all my homies, including my family. You just get caught up in living the day-to-day grind. When I did go home, I loved the get-togethers. Something was missing: ME. Where did I go? I was wrapped up in the new life I made and emotionally left everyone else behind. I didn't realize the empty place in my heart was the real void of the familiarity of family and the friends with whom I had been raised.

Of course, I would never regret moving. I had to step out of my comfort zone to create a life in the South. I had to grow and change, which may have not occurred if I stayed in Boston. Looking back, I would have liked to been more involved with my girlfriends as they had their babies. I would have enjoyed them really getting to know my kids. In fact, I needed them and my family for support. I didn't have to be lonely even though I was alone in Georgia.

Now that my kids are a bit older, I can take a weekend here and there and come to Boston to reconnect. Every summer I spend a week or two in Maine with my besties and our kids. These are memories I will take to the grave. I cherish every moment I get with my family and friends from Boston. More recently, I have even reconnected with other high school friends who are so wonderful! When I was a student, I was too wrapped up in my own lack of self-esteem to break out of my shell to reach out to these beautiful people.

This weekend, I came back to Boston for a disco bash and reunion hosted by an old friend. Of course, my besties were right there with me dancing to the sounds of the 70's and 80's under the disco ball. I met up with so many old friends, people I don't remember not knowing. I spent time with my high school friends, an afternoon with my aunt and breakfast with my best girl, Dana. My sister even poked her head out for a bit.

Make new friends, but keep the old. One is silver and the other, gold. I'll say my old friends are platinum, gems to be cherished. I miss them dearly, and I know I will never let go of the life and memories we hold together. You know, I have always had the ruby slippers on: "There's no place like home!"

I've Got a Meeting in the Ladies' Room

I'll be back real soon...What actually goes on behind the closed doors of the powder room? The conversations and events in the lavatory are relative to the establishment. The more upscale a venue is, the nicer the bathrooms. The guests typically follow suit. I've noticed, though, some things never change. Here's my chronology of bathroom behavior, at least for the egg-producing portion of society:

For wee little chicks, the bathroom is a playground. It is here we search the cabinets for our mom's toiletries, where we can only imagine the secret world of the grown-up girl with the same parts, only bigger and hairier (it was the pre-Brazilian days). What are these tubes filled with cotton balls? Instinctively we knew it was for the "restricted basement" area. We splashed on the Jean Nate and Charlie to smell like mom. It was the days when my sister and I were afraid to take a bath fearing Jaws would erupt from the drain. In school, we would congregate in the bathroom to get the 411 on the neighborhood. We may even get silly, throw water and make soap bubbles. No matter which bathroom, ultimately, an adult would be screaming to clean up the mess and get out.

As puberty arrived, the interest in the Kotex and Tampax piqued. When would I need these? What is this K-Y for? "How long will you be in there? I need to go." Sorry sister, the days of sharing the toilet are over. Squatter's rights. I am the queen of the latrine for now. This was the only privacy I had. At least I could get away from the insanity and dive into my own world in the quiet of my shower and personal pampering. Now school was a different story. The girls' room was the place to be if you wanted to know who was kissing whom. What is French kissing? I always felt left out since I wasn't kissing anybody, nor did I have the opportunity. Some girl was always crying, bitching or fighting in the girls' room. Then the make-up hug came with continued tears. Oh no! Blood on my Catholic school skirt....where's my mother's Kotex? Here comes Sister Lorraine (the bitch who hit kids)..."What's going on here? Get back to class before I call Father McClaughlin."

During high school, the bathroom at home was an area that my father avoided while my sister and I were around. God forbid he caught us running to the shower in a towel holding the box of "tampoons" (his name for them). He'd let out a shriek and run the other way. During the school day, the lav was the place to make a safe change before the Catholic skirt stain (I got smarter.). Now that everyone knew how to French kiss, besides me, the subject matter progressed. The topic became the dating scene. The cutest boys, the football players and the cheerleaders always seemed to be dating. I never had anything to contribute to these conversations. The only activity for me, besides pad swapping, was trying to sneak a smoke before the bathroom lady came back. Once a week, a cat fight would break out. Someone called someone's mother a douche bag and it was over. The F-word was flying, and sometimes even a few fists, too. Oh no! Here comes Sister Catherine McGary, appropriately nicknamed "The Walrus." "Get back to class or see me in detention! Does anyone smell smoke?"

The college dorm changed my bathroom behavior. I could smoke in my room, so the bathroom was a place for hygiene and having to learn how to poop with someone six inches away. I think this is where I developed my fear of going #2 outside my house and developed the need for Metamucil. More importantly, the bar and nightclub powder rooms opened my eyes to a whole new world. The lines were long. Hurry, I needed to re-apply my lipstick and get back to my fav song and the cute guy who might just give me the time of day this time. Once inside, the conversation again progressed to who was sleeping with whom. Ugh! I had nothing to contribute. Why was the mirror off the wall? The girls with the straws and white stuff on their noses needed it for a close up. Is that girl a diabetic? Why would she inject insulin between her toes? It didn't take long for me to realize what was really going on. Not to mention, there was the potential for a cat fight. There was always some bitching going on. Some douche was sleeping with someone's drunk boyfriend...here we go again!

It must be noted that it was in these days that I (and every other full-bladdered chick) would use the men's room to avoid the line. I did, once, pee on Revere Beach with at least five others after the candy man visited Regis College and we needed a Kelly's Roast Beef fix to satiate the munchies, the one very rare time that I was actually bad.

I now share my bathroom with my husband. To my chagrin, our four boys love my bathroom, even though they each have their own. "Mom, are you done? I want to take a shower!" This is my bathroom! "Sooo what!" Fast forward to my forties, where I frequent upscale restaurants as well as my fav ATL hot spots. My youngest came out of the men's room at New York Prime

saying"Mom, did you have mouthwash and lotion in yours?" The

ladies are sweet and reserved with their minks and Chanel lipstick.

 Just down the road is my go-to nightclub, Rose Bar, where the

bathroom lady passes me a paper towel and says, "Hey baby, where

you been?" The girls are crowded in, applying their makeup for the

ultimate pickup. So I drop $5 in the tip bucket and move out for the

younger girls to discuss the night's prospects. It's just not the same

here in ATL. I'll wait to go home to Boston and hit a club with my

besties for an old school meeting in the ladies' room.

<u>You're Gonna Make It After All!</u>

Last week my husband called me as I was leaving a doctor's appointment with one of our boys. He said, "Am I on speaker?" I knew something was up, and a sick feeling came over me. I said, "No." He proceeded to tell me one of our other boys was in a car accident, and he's ok. I sighed with relief and listened to the details.

Later I called my son and told him, no matter what, as long as he's ok, we can deal with anything. His safety and well-being were more important to us than any car. I found myself choked up and tearing up, even though I wasn't emotional at all a few minutes earlier. But the truth does this. The reality that my boys' lives are my priority evoked my mother-heart to spill over with uncontrollable feeling. It's all going to be ok.

As I approach my 46th birthday, I find myself reflecting on the progress I have made in my personal journey, and what it has meant for me and the people around me. The obstacles I have faced had, at one point or another, seemed insurmountable. Most of the pit stops on my path largely entailed looking in the mirror, going inside, facing myself, the good, the bad and the ugly. It was at these moments I knew something wasn't quite right. I was not happy.

What was holding me back from enjoying my life?

Facing myself was so scary. I realized that whatever I was doing, whatever my behavior, reaction to my environment, anger at the people in my world, was a direct result of me not being true to myself. I was not living as a gift to the world, but was hiding behind some façade of what I thought the world wanted from me. As I continued in my Bizarro bubble, I became more unsettled and agitated.

What to do? I have this tremendous desire to experience life to its fullest, to be truly joyful and happy...the real McCoy for me. I wanted honest felicity. So I had to face my demon of the day, whatever was disrupting my spirit. This is where we decide either to step into the ring and fight or watch the excitement from the audience. This is the deciding point: I could either sweep it all under the rug and continue my charade or confront my junk. I just couldn't keep pretending. I took the first long look into the mirror and resolved to make the necessary changes and attitude adjustments, no matter how dreadful.

People can say how courageous this may have been and will be as I continue to peel the layers away. I don't call it courage. It's more the desire to delight in all that God has given me. It's an insatiable quest for wholeness that encompasses all that surrounds me. I want this more than I fear the challenge of facing myself.

I know many of you say you cannot do it. You may even believe you have nothing to change, which is a great place to be. I tell you, you will be happier and more peaceful if you just look in the mirror. If I did it, you can. My words to you are the same as the ones to my son: "It's all going to be ok." And from the theme to Mary Tyler Moore: "Who can turn the world on with her smile? You're gonna make it after all!"

A Special Birthday Blog

A few years back I was using St. Francis de Sales' book, "Introduction to the Devout Life" for meditation. The first topic, from which ultimately I could not advance, was pondering on my own life. The article encouraged thanking God for creating me, breathing life into me, allowing me to exist. Well, I thought, what's the big deal? Why should I thank God? What was so great about me? Is the world any better with me around? What if I didn't exist? Maybe everyone would be better for it. Was I a burden? Did I make that much of a difference? I mean, who really cares if I am here or not?

I brought these thoughts to my priest. Here's what he said: "That is the most stupid thing God has ever heard!" I started to laugh (excuse my sick humor). No matter what he said, I couldn't shake this thought. What value am I to God and to the people around me?

Does anyone else think about this stuff? Am I alone in wondering "Why the Hell am I here?" Do I serve a purpose? Why is this even important to me? My reasons are two-fold. I never considered myself worth it. As a young person, I never felt I was worth the effort for Prince Charming to come rescue me from my dreaded self. I was not pretty enough, smart enough and whole enough that anyone should make an effort. As I managed a house and four kids, I put everyone's needs before my own. I denied myself basic needs unnecessarily.

Also, I have this desire to make a difference. There is something inside me that yearns to influence people and society. I want to make a positive impact on the people in my path. I want them to know I love them unconditionally. I wish to dig into anyone's heart and find out what makes them tick. I don't know why, but this is my motivation for most everything I do.

So here I am on my birthday revisiting why God willed me into being. Although I no longer go to the place where I am not worth God's or anyone else's effort, I do long to make a difference with you and the world. At the risk of sounding mushy: I really do love the people in my life, and there's room for more. So when I say at the end of each blog "tell me what's going on in your life," I mean it.

So I say to myself today, "Happy Birthday, Just Steph. God loves you and so do others."

Let's Shake on It

A friend called me the other night asking if I had a minute to talk. We had discussed previously how we both suffer with the fear of public humiliation. She wanted to discuss this on a deeper level knowing my story and my everyday struggles. She asked, "How do you get over the fear?" I said, "You don't." What you want to do, whatever you desire to accomplish must outweigh the fear. The scary event before you must be part of your journey. This is what you are meant to do. You have a purpose. This purpose gives you the courage to catapult you over the fear, through the experience to the other side where your true self shines its beauty to the world.

I was born in the days before ultrasound. So I was a surprise to my parents when I emerged from the safety of my mother's womb into the cruel world with a small right hand that was without all its digits. I know that sounds so angry. But that's what the world used to be for me: scary and unsafe. My close-knit Italian family, filled with aunts, uncles, cousins and eggplant parm, provided a secure cocoon where I could whack each of them with my little hand and no one flinched. But beyond the smell of baked ziti was a world filled with mean kids and curious onlookers.

I was the last one to tie my shoes in school; I had to ask the teacher. I rarely participated in organized sports: it was too embarrassing to switch my softball glove to throw the ball back, not to mention too slow. So what did I do to feel better? I ate and surrounded myself with only the people I trusted with my life and my hand. I grew in a way that now seems sideways, becoming more self-conscious and less active. My constant companions became the characters from Happy Days, Laverne & Shirley & Welcome Back, Kotter. This is why I can sing every theme song from the seventies and early eighties TV shows on a drop of a dime.

My adolescence and early twenties were more of the same. The nightclub scene was a walk through the lion's den. I had lost some weight, but I still had a small hand. I would meet guys in a club, introduce myself and they would just walk away. I became the world's greatest manipulator of my surroundings. I could strategically place myself anywhere in a room, church or club where I could avoid shaking too many people's hands, and I especially avoided children. Kids are the worst...they scream out loud, "WHAT HAPPENED TO YOU? MOM, DID YOU SEE HER?"

Fast forward to my forties. A husband, four kids and many years of therapy later, I knew I wasn't happy. I am an extrovert. I gain energy by being around people and interacting. I love getting to know them. I love meeting new people, which means at some point shaking a new person's hand. I attend church every Sunday. Every Sunday I think about scouting out the pews for the least amount of kids in the area and usher my family in. This is no way to live.

I never even really talked about it with my closest friends. I became the great pretender as well. There has always been another elephant in the room that we didn't address. So along with therapy, I started boxing in 2008. It was in the ring that I gained the confidence I needed to wrestle my demons?. I used my wraps to help me jump rope and I can finally do push-ups and dips. I put on the gloves, and I am like everyone else.

I took off the weight and tried really hard to stop manipulating my surroundings. I thank God for my challenges. What doesn't kill you makes you stronger. I am the stronger person for it. The world is no longer cruel; it is my playground. Every day is tough. The fear never leaves me. The sting of people's first reaction to me can still be sharp. But this is my purpose, to show the world what it means to truly step out of your shell and shine your

beautiful true self. This is the gift in you and me that the world is

awaiting. I don't want to let you all down by keeping me hidden.

 Your true self is your gift to the world! Let it shine and let's shake

on it, or just give me a

hug.

One Bad Apple Don't Spoil the Whole Bunch, Steph

Give it one more try before I give up on love. Putting ourselves out there and living a truly authentic life is dangerous. Love is a battlefield, inside and out. We are vulnerable. Our hearts are on the line. I have heard the lamentations of so many friends who refuse to step out of their comfort zone for themselves or another out of fear of being hurt. What is at stake? As high rollers in the game of life and love, we gamble with rejection, humiliation, abandonment, frustration and a hard look in the mirror on the wall.

What are the actual risks? Is what I fear probable? Remember, the feelings are valid, but they are an indicator that something, some past occurrence, is controlling our perspective on an event. In short, our memories and previous experiences, accurate or not, affect how we behave. For me, how people have reacted toward me and my small right hand has shaped how I feel about meeting new people. I also suffer with a sense of shame about not looking perfect (my small hand, a bad hair day, a zit on my face, etc.) or when I make even minor mistakes; you know, being human.

Recently I have had a few memories come back to me that were quite painful. My current situation caused an eruption in my brain where these events spewed forth from the depths of my

subconscious like an undiscovered volcano. Why now? I believe it

is two-fold. As I journey toward my own sense of balance and

peace, I find myself venturing out of my comfort zone. I am really

challenging myself both physically and emotionally. A subject that I

pretended didn't exist has become a topic of conversation for me.

Talking to my family, close friends and trainers about my hand, my

feelings and physical limitations has caused a major tremor within

my psyche.

In addition, my authenticity lies in my extroverted

personality. I love people. I love meeting new people. I long to hear

their hearts, know what makes them tick. But, and that's a an upper-

case BUT, my unpleasant life experiences have caused me to project

onto all of you how you will treat me. Unbeknownst to me, I have

been hiding my true self from all of you and the world out of fear

that you will not like me, find me ugly or laugh at me. Sounds

juvenile, and it is. It comes from what I believed about myself after

only a few ugly encounters. Most of my life has been filled with

laughter, joy of life, beautiful friends and family and even kind

strangers. Unfortunately, for all of you I haven't met, and even some of you I already know, I have preconceived notions as to how you will treat me. I have judged you all unfairly, made you out to be unkind, mean and cold.

Flooded by memories and determined to change my personal reality, I have re-evaluated my misconceptions of how people perceive me. I am working toward not formulating biased opinions. What I really want is to be free of these judgments in order to be my authentic self and love you all as you are, not as I think you are. I can finally tell myself: one bad apple don't spoil the whole bunch, Steph.

You are not what happened to you in the past. You are now, you are this moment. What will you do with it? Who will you choose to become?

I Did It My Way...

"Regrets, I have a few; but then, again, too few to mention..."
Some years back I attended a series of talks on finding and doing
God's will in my life. The person speaking began with a negative
criticism of Frank Sinatra's "My Way." I'm already pissed off. You
never insult Ol' Blue Eyes to Italians. The Chairman of the Board
can do no wrong in our minds. So what was his gripe with "My
Way?"

In a nutshell, the speaker maintained that when Frankie
promoted his way, it was not God's way. Essentially, when we do it
our way, it is not according to God's will for us. In some cases, this
may be true. BUT, as I continue to look inward, find balance,
acknowledge my dreams and live them out, I realize that "my way"
IS God's way. I am not referring here to just doing whatever feels
good at anybody's expense. I am talking about that which is
embedded within.

My dreams, desires, everything that floats my boat, has been
placed within me by God. Two of the fruits of the Holy Spirit are
joy and peace. I am most at peace when I am fulfilling my deepest
aspirations and my longings. I am excited at the thought of doing

every day what I love most, what makes me happy. Does God's will have to be misery? There is only one entity that wants us to be miserable. You know who that is.

Search deep within. Do it your way and know this about me: **"Yes, there were times, I'm sure you knew/When I bit off more than I could chew/But through it all, when there was doubt/I ate it up and spit it out/I faced it all and I stood tall and did it my way."**

Just Steph Today

It has taken many years of therapy, coaching and the school of hard knocks to get to where I am today. Supportive family and friends along with my loyal readers aided the healing process. I can attest to the darkest hour occurring just before dawn. Although I have been self-examining for many years, it took serious life issues to bring forth real change.

I finally feel secure in my own skin. I continue to strive for balance in the four aspects of the human person. I also do a lot of self-talk. I talk myself through situations that continue to be uncomfortable. I also express and validate my feelings. For example, I couldn't perform a triceps exercise a few weeks ago. Instead of stuffing it and pretending, I shed a few quiet tears. My trainer asked what was wrong. I told him I get frustrated when I cannot do what everyone else is doing. This is real progress for me. Hopefully, I will get to the place where I just do some other comparable move without a lump in my throat.

I have started my own business, Just Steph, LLC. I am no longer hiding behind managing the kids and the house. Atlanta offers many opportunities to network. I am getting out there, telling my story and meeting a variety of individuals. My ultimate goal is to have my own radio and or television talk show while continuing to write and speak. I long for the day when everyone will have heard my story. I will update my talks to include what I have learned as I build a successful company.

This last section includes one of my favorite chapters about my first networking event. I have also included my biography, references and information on my products. Please feel free to contact me at steph@juststeph.com with any questions or comments about my book. I would love to hear your story as well. Email me!

__Just Steph Works Hard for the Money__

Just about every weekend for the last three years, I have frequented my fav Atlanta restaurants, piano bars and nightclubs. More often than not, my husband and I eat at the bar accompanied by ATL's finest mixologists and regular barflies. I stand piano side singing along to the tunes that everyone knows, like "Brandy" or my girlfriend and I shake our booties to the likes of "Call Me Maybe." At all these venues, I can work the room. I meet people, dig into their lives, find out what makes them tick. When I see them at a later date, I tap into my memory and retell them their story.

This is baffling to my weekend acquaintances, especially since vodka is usually involved. But this is what I do and do best. I bring out people's hearts. I love it and don't even realize it until a second or third chance encounter, when I experience their emotion when we talk.

After raising my family for 20-plus years, I am getting back into the work world. Doing what I do best, telling my story, hearing about all of yours, finding humor in most everything and teaching balance in life are my passions. Through keynote speaking, workshops, life coaching and eventually a radio and/or TV talk show, I hope to, at some point, forge a career. So I decided to attend an after-hours social networking group. I harassed my printer to have my newest business cards ready, chose my outfit, swallowed my fear and jumped into the passenger seat so my husband could coach and escort me.

With my salad in my throat, I reluctantly strolled into the hip ATL venue at which I spent my last two Saturday dinners. We donned our name tags and dropped our business cards into the fish bowl for a door prize. Of course, I was stumbling. This was my first business card drive-by. My husband is a construction executive. The first guy we met was a construction litigation lawyer. Then the event organizer comes by to greet us. Unable to stop myself, I proceed to bring up irrelevant sh*t as my husband is hand signaling me to STFU (SHUT THE F#$k UP). Then comes the moment for the drawing, and guess who wins the two bottles of Russian Vodka not currently available in the US? You've got it...husband #1!

I did get to meet a local meteorologist who was darling and Miss Georgia USA. Maybe they will get me a gig somewhere. Who knows? But I'm heading out tonight to try again. If nothing else, I get to give out my business cards again tonight to executives

interested in my husband's business. I'll keep you posted.

She Let Go

"Without a thought or word, she let go. She let go of the fear. She let go of the judgments. She let go of the confluence of opinions swarming around her head. She let go of the committee of indecision within her. She let go of all the right reasons. Wholly and completely, without hesitation or worry, she just let go. She let go of all the memories that held her back. She let go of all the anxiety that kept her from moving forward. She let go of all the planning and all of the calculations about how to do it just right. She didn't promise to let go. She didn't write the projected date in her day planner. She made no public announcement or put an ad in the newspaper. She didn't check the weather report or read her daily horoscope. She just let go. She didn't analyze it, and she didn't call her friends to discuss it. She didn't call the prayer line. She didn't utter one word. She just let go. No one was around when it happened. There was no applause: no congratulations. No one thanked her or praised her. No one noticed a thing. Like a leaf falling from a tree, she just let go. There was no effort; there was no struggle. It wasn't good; it wasn't bad. It was what it was, and it is just that. In the space of letting go, she let it be. A small smile came over her face…a light breeze blew through her. And the sun shone,

and the moon rose."

- Ernest Holmes

Steph's Biography

For over 20 years, Steph has managed a home and family while on a path to physical, spiritual, emotional and intellectual well-being. Through personal trials, she came to understand that only through significant changes in these four aspects could she experience peace.

Steph was raised in an Italian neighborhood in the Boston suburbs, and her upbringing provided a rich source of experiences. She earned a B.A. in Management and a certificate in Communications from Regis College in Weston, MA.

Her ethnicity brought with it as much pain as joy in her life. There was a tremendous emphasis on food that contributed to her being overweight. Steph is challenged with a physical disability that added to her feelings of rejection and loneliness, a misunderstanding of God and her faith and not acknowledging and nourishing her intellect and talents.

Today, Steph has journeyed uphill to make strides in maintaining balance and peace in her life with a specific emphasis on physical health. She is a proponent of healthy relationships and working toward continual personal growth spiritually and intellectually. In addition to providing group and private life coaching on the four aspects of the human person, Steph offers keynote speaking, half-day workshops, radio and TV guest spots and article contributions for your publication.

She co-hosts a web talk show with comedian Charlene Mae, www.thestephandcharshow.com

Watch her on YouTube, http://www.youtube.com/user/theonlywayisupbaby1, demonstrating cooking and health tips. For more information, browse Steph's website, www.juststeph.com or contact her via email at steph@juststeph.com.

Just Steph Products

- **Private and Group Life Coaching** – Through discussions and journaling, we will work towards balancing the four aspects of the human person. Steph will bring her experiences and expertise on balancing life and growing comfortable in your own skin to a small group setting. Simultaneously, you will reap the benefits of discussion, peer suggestions and support. Group sessions will occur in a series of six gatherings with a minimum of four participants and a maximum of eight. The session will last for one hour, and will meet twice a month in the evening for three months.

• **Keynote Speaking** –Steph is available to inspire your group with her uplifting life story that chronicles what it means to truly be comfortable in one's own skin. Her determination to overcome a physical handicap and the desire for acceptance from the people in her path catapulted her into a fight for self-love and personal success.

• **Half-Day Workshops-** Steph will integrate her personal journey with strategies to achieve balance in the four aspects of the human person: physical, emotional, spiritual and intellectual into a half-day workshop. During your time with Steph, you and your group will gain a better perspective on your lives, how to live a more peaceful existence and advance toward self-love and true joy.

• **Radio/TV Guest Spots** - "Just Steph Live" will enhance your talk show or discussion topics relating to health, wellness and finding humor in difficult life situations. Once they experience her, your audience will be calling for more of Just Steph.

Praise and Recommendations for Just Steph

"This is one incredible woman – smart, funny and inspiring. Her amazing talent of humor and her unique way with words will lift you over your obstacles. Steph is a beautiful person inside and out. You will be better for having worked with her or heard her speak."

Debbie Brown, Executive Coach D & B Consulting

"Steph has shown an unwavering commitment to fitness, which is one example of her many accomplishments since she began training with me September 2008. Since then, Steph has not just lost those last ten pounds, she has toned, gotten stronger and has mastered exercises she never thought were physically possible for her. Her self-confidence and motivation to continue to pursue physical wellness has skyrocketed. She has demonstrated the determination and desire to excel at the gym as though she was preparing for a main event bout at the MGM Grand Casino. Steph is committed to her own health and is always interested in promoting a healthy lifestyle to other gym members.

Steph has been an inspiration to me and the many other gym members who have gotten to know her these past four years. It's been an honor and privilege to call her my pugilist, and I enjoy having her as part of the Delgado Boxing family!"

Paul Delgado, Director of Operations / Trainer Delgado Boxing

"I have attended Steph's cooking classes. Her energy and enthusiasm make the time go so quickly that you're sorry to see it end. She is so organized. She makes whatever she does seem easy. Her ability to instill confidence makes you believe that working with her will allow you to achieve your goals."

Debbie Bottner Studio Printing

"I have observed Steph immerse herself in her journey; she is both an enthusiastic student and teacher. She approaches everything she does with determination and vigor and is a wonderful motivator. Steph enjoys an excellent reputation among her friends and colleagues, and is looked upon as a leader in nearly everything she becomes involved with. Her cooking classes are well planned, and she is at ease in front of a camera or large crowd. Steph is hard working and a credit to our community, and I highly recommend her."

Sharon Crippen-Ginsburg

"Throughout the last twelve years, I have known Steph to be the type of person who provides a positive perspective and humor to every situation she experiences. Tenacious in her role to raise her four boys, her drive, motivation, faith and sense of humor are the foundation for her successes in life. Selfless as she is, it was not until her boys were situated full time in school that she looked inward and began to focus on the next phase her life, using these same skills to transform herself and others around her. Steph's amazing sense of humor buffers the most difficult of situations and often offers relief to the more serious stories in her blog. She has an amazing network of friends and followers who count on her honesty and loyalty. I congratulate Steph for her many accomplishments, both personal and professional, and wish her the very best."

Jamie Arthur, PhD

"I enlisted Steph as a life coach to lose weight and change my eating habits. I ended up getting that and so much more! Stephanie is one of those rare people who are in the perfect job for her. She is an excellent motivator, listener, organizer, advisor, and wellness and well-being expert. And she makes you laugh while doing it all!

I am not new to fitness and nutrition. I was stuck in some decades-long habits and attitudes that were hindering me from moving forward and liking my life and myself. Some of them I was aware of, some not. The most prominent one when I first contacted Steph was that I was repeatedly dependent upon diet pills to get past my plateau. With Just Steph, I was able to reach my ideal weight in 6 weeks with nothing but all-natural real food (that I enjoy) for the first time in years.

I can't recommend Just Steph enough. She was a mini-miracle for me. Stephanie has made a big difference in my life, and she will not disappoint!

Gena Middleton, Life Coaching Client

Made in the USA
Charleston, SC
18 May 2013